The Beau

A Celebration of Teenage Life and Faith

By Peter Tassi

In memory of my beautiful nephew Carson Dale Blake, who lit up every room and every heart with his wonderful and radiant smile.

Living the Good News
    a division of The Morehouse Group
Editorial Offices
600 Grant Street, Suite 400
Denver, CO 80203

James R. Creasey, Publisher

Dirk deVries, Editor
Jim Lemons, Layout
Val Price, Cover Design
Printed in the United States of America

ISBN 1-889108-49-9

Table of Contents

Foreword

> "Work is love made visible."
> — Kahlil Gibran

Both in his work as a high school chaplain and in the case studies he presents in this book, Peter Tassi embodies Gibran's challenging observation—*love made visible*. While many social workers, advocates or care-givers eventually become emotionally detached from their clients and succumb to burnout, Peter finds inspiration and great joy—even personal rejuvenation—in the struggles, the dreams, the small or distant victories of those who seek his counsel. His empathy is matched by his contagious enthusiasm in sharing the yoke of those around him who are troubled in any way. As one reads his accounts of marginalized heroes, one realizes that Peter can uncover the good news about anyone, and to use this revelation to begin the process of healing, to ignite the spark of hope, to inspire the journey toward the achievement of dreams.

I first met Peter when we were assigned to the same school, he as the chaplain and I as the principal. We shared our visions, which were similar, and our plans for achieving our goals. I failed to realize how much Peter loved a challenge! I suggested we spruce up the school chapel on a limited budget to make it a more inviting place for prayer and worship. He immediately recruited his friends, sought expert input, worked feverishly and completely overhauled the chapel, changing it into a place of magnificent simplicity...all for less than three hundred dollars. Peter often became so engrossed in the task, painting and manufacturing his own artistic contributions to this project, that security patrols questioned his overnight presence in the building.

I also suggested to Peter that he might initiate a few projects to implement our school's mandate to promote Catholic social teachings. Throughout the year, Peter activated a *large* group of students to raise a *great* deal of money for local charities. He chose less-recognized students and gave them the opportunity to become organizers, leaders and prophets. These teens blossomed in their confidence and self-esteem, even as Peter remained humbly in the background. His concern was not for the accolades that accompany a successful project, but for the spiritual and emotional growth of those teens who brought compassion, dedication and talents to carry each project to completion. This pastoral dimension reflects Peter's style in dealing with *all* the people he serves each day.

Peter's background and character provide him with unique skills for his role and a wide-ranging perspective as an author. From a no-nonsense, steeltown father with a heart of gold, Peter inherited an incredible work ethic. The high school football field and the boxing rings of his hometown forged his strength. Conversely, his seminary training and early career as a high school teacher produced pastoral sensitivity. Most important, Peter's understanding of teenagers results from his most significant role, that of a father accompanying his own children through the trials of adolescence.

Peter's empathy flows from the personal struggles of his own journey. He has travelled the fast track of the entertainment industry, developed the passion of an artist and cultivated his obsession to write. His autobiography could be a bestseller, yet, in true form, he chooses to write about others—those whom he has helped from despair, fear and darkness and elevated to undreamt levels of confidence and self-acceptance. Furthermore, he chooses not to sensationalize their situations, but to let them teach and inspire others. He is the ultimate altruist in every facet of his life.

The characters in Peter's stories are not fictionalized, nor are his emotions or advice embellished. Perhaps this explains why the accounts hit home with such impact. We are put in the chaplain's chair, we see and hear what he sees and hears, and we feel his emotions. Real life is far more gripping than a contrived story. Real love finds a route from the keyboard to the reader. While Peter's insights and advice to his reading audience are awesome, his love for others and his passion for helping are of greater significance to those of us who have the privilege of working with teenagers, who so cherish this love and respect.

This book will be of great value to those who work or live with teenagers for two reasons. First, it kindles in the reader feelings of love, sympathy, hope, desperation, guilt, perseverance and victory. Second, it offers logical, practical advice written by an understanding and thoughtful advocate for teens. Their stories not only underlie the author's wisdom and suggestions, but also prove the credibility of his convictions. Most teenagers have a difficult time verbalizing their feelings and motivations in the vernacular of adults. Peter, however, becomes the master translator in telling us not only what they feel, but also why they feel that way and how

we adults can respond. Most problems in human relationships stem from a lack of communication; this book, in many
ways, serves to bridge the gap between adult and teen by
improving our understanding of adolescent emotions.

In daring to share his feelings, experiences and stories, Peter
enriches the minds and hearts of all those in relationship
with teenagers—parents, teachers, mentors, friends. His message is simple: love, respect and understanding are absolute
necessities for the survival of a child. The task for teachers
and parents is in learning how to show this love, how to
demonstrate this respect and how to act on this understanding. This book goes a long way in teaching us these things.

John Valvasori, Principal
St. Thomas More Secondary School
Hamilton, Ontario

Introduction

Life often misleads us. We look for treasures in the wrong place, and what we often perceive as a treasure is not a treasure at all. Our greatest treasure sits around us in church, crowds the hallways and classrooms of our schools and lives with us in our homes. It is not our status in life, the possessions we have or the money we make; it is the children—those we lead, those we teach, those we parent. They are our greatest treasures, true miracles, gifts given us by God, a source of happiness, love and fulfillment.

Society frequently devalues teenagers, sometimes even viewing them as obstacles to adult freedom and happiness. Teens are often viewed as "less than"—less intelligent, less spiritual, less prudent, less wise, weaker. How far from the truth! On the contrary, teens are an untapped resource of great spirituality, strength, sensibility and wisdom.

We look to TV evangelists, local pastors, friends and all sorts of gurus for answers to life's tough questions and the wisdom, insight and strength to deal with life's difficulties. *Why not look to our own teenagers?* Sit with them. Talk with them. Reach out to them for help. Listen. You will discover how much they have to offer. Their advice is simple...but profound. They approach life clearly, unmuddled by the trappings of the adult world. They feel acutely the suffering of others; they genuinely love others. Add to this their endless willingness to give. Turn to teenagers, and you will be amazed at what they have to offer.

I consider it a great honor to have worked with teens over the years. It took me a long time to find this place of gratitude where I am now, but the search was well worth it. Working with teenagers has filled my life with profound experiences. They have helped me to see God more clearly and have brought me closer to God. I am grateful to them and hope that my work with them has been as much a reward to them as it has been to me.

I can never convey all the wonderful experiences I have had with teens, nor all that I have learned from them. I have, however, collected some of these treasured experiences and offer them in this book. I hope, through this book, that you see the beauty in our teenagers, and that you find some helpful hints in working and living with them.

1: Big John's Story

Big John walked in, only in ninth grade and already six feet tall. In spite of his intimidating size and his rough appearance, he had a baby face, a smile that would calm a lion, and eyes that sparkled with hope. Little did I realize then how profoundly he would influence my life.

Originally from Florida, John had been abandoned by his parents, left to grow up on the streets. He made his way through the United States and then to Canada. His pilgrimage led him on many detours, including gang life and petty crime, but I could tell from our first visit that Big John was determined to make something more of his life. There was something special about this boy: although hardened by his experiences, he held a surprisingly positive attitude toward life.

In Canada, John qualified for welfare and moved into his own apartment. He attended school and was a real asset to our football program. However, the tough life he had was not about to end. He struggled with academics, found it difficult to make close friends whom he could trust, and struggled to survive financially on the money provided by welfare.

At times I would slip him a few dollars, but as his debts increased I went to Frank, our principal, for help. Frank would always find money for any student in need; there was an unspoken understanding between us—he would produce the money and I wouldn't ask where it came from.

In the next few years, Big John developed into a great football player and a dedicated student. Academics never came easily, but he never gave up. His physical growth, in contrast, *did* come easily; his appetite was as large as he was and he seemed to get bigger by the day. Loving teachers and our viceprincipal often brought him food packages.

Frank continued providing money. As difficult as times were, John kept his faith, believed in himself, remained focused and offered a smile to everyone. In spite of his hard life, he demonstrated a deep spirituality. His hope was fostered and kept alive by many loving and caring staff at the school.

Eventually John's financial situation became desperate. Unless he could share expenses with others, surviving on welfare was impossible. He fell behind in his rent and never had enough money to feed his ravenous appetite. We investigated other possibilities and eventually found John a place to live at a nearby youth home.

This home is the last chance for many kids who live on the streets. Although the home was full, they agreed to furnish an extra room in the basement to accommodate this friendly giant. John no longer had to worry about rent, food, transportation and moral support. He could now focus completely on his studies and football.

As graduation approached, John returned to my office. Almost five years had passed since our first meeting. He now stood six foot six and weighed about 285 pounds—a mountain of a man who melted you with his baby face and million dollar smile. He told me that an American university was interested in giving him a scholarship but he did not have the money to take the required exams. Once again I visited Frank's office and without hesitation he wrote a check to pay for the exams.

Three weeks later John returned to my office. I will never forget that meeting and the conversation that we had. Somewhat humbled and perhaps a little shamed, John said in a soft voice, "Sir, I failed the exams."

I immediately responded, "That's okay, John, what are our options now?" I sounded calm but remember feeling panic inside. I wasn't sure of what the options were and was fearful that this would eliminate the chance of his university scholarship. All I could think of was how far he had come and how dreadful it would be if he had to give it all up.

My anxieties were quickly put to rest when he replied, "I can write them again, sir, but I need more money, and I don't know where I will get it from." I hesitated for a moment and felt the relief that came with knowing he had another chance. Just as I was about to respond with excitement and confirmation, John jumped in with an eager and desperate addition that he had to share with me. "There is something else I want to tell you sir."

"What is it?" I asked.

"I have turned my life over to Christ, and there is nothing that will stop me now."

I took a deep breath and felt renewed energy. I quickly replied, "I've been waiting a long time to hear you talk like that, John. However, it's money you need right now for those exams, and it's Frank and not Christ who signs the checks." We laughed together, and, with humble hearts, we made our way back to Frank's office like two poor beggars.

Frank did indeed write another check. And Big John passed the exams. He won a full four-year scholarship (valued at $120,000) to a renowned American university.

Big John's story inspires me. Think about what he had to overcome. His parents abandoned him. He was in a foreign country with no place to live, no food and no money. By our standards he had nothing. But really Big John had everything, because Big John had his dignity, his pride, his faith, a dream to hold on to and a lot of heart.

The hidden beauty in this young, nomadic boy shone brilliantly, yet few could see it. This same beauty shines in so many of our teens, lost on the streets. Where it comes from, how it got there, I don't know, but if we look, we always find it buried deep inside.

Thank you, Lord, for giving to this world such a beautiful young man. Thank you, Lord, for all those who believed in Big John and helped him make the impossible possible.
Amen.

Quick Tips

- When assessing a teen's potential—looking for the beauty within—see beyond life situation and appearance, beyond the immediate and external, to the inner self and all its possibilities.
- No matter how many times teens disappoint you, be there to help them back on their feet.
- Do slow to judge teenagers' spirituality based only on external behavior. God lives inside, perhaps most visible in the their desire to make something good of their lives.
- Use humor when relating to teens. Humor builds relationships.

2: Our Goal—To Walk With Them

Big John's story testifies to the determination, faith, strength and inner beauty that exist in teenagers. He demonstrates that any obstacle can be overcome, and that, with the help of others, the dreams of teenagers can become reality.

"Big Johns" surround you. In this book, I invite you to "walk with them," discovering for yourself their inner strength and beauty. You will read of teenagers who overcame insurmountable odds to find meaning and joy in their lives. You will be surprised at the wonderful gifts that they possess, and the gift they are to us. Even the roughest and toughest teenagers have within them a deep spirituality and the ability to give great things to society.

I have three hopes for this book:

First, I hope that through this book you will believe, as I do, that *no teenager is unreachable*. We are often surprised by the accomplishments of those teens from whom we expect the least. You will discover that they have simple but wonderful dreams, that what they want from life is often different from what we think they want. You will understand their hunger to be accepted, affirmed and loved by the adult world. You will hear them as they cry out to us to help them make their dreams come true.

Second, I hope that through this book I will *dispel many of the myths and misconceptions about teenagers*. They are not an aggressive, loud and vulgar generation wrapped up in materialism, negativity and promiscuity. On the contrary, they are a people with a burning desire to love and be loved, to bring peace to a chaotic world, to help those in need and to live a simple, secure, spiritual and productive life. Travel with me along this road and enter this wonderful world—their world.

Third, I also hope that this book makes clear *some of what causes the insecurity and pain in the life of our teens and how we can help them overcome these obstacles.* I believe it provides sound advice that will help you as a parent, counselor or educator in your work with teens.

Where do we start? With the belief that each and every teenager is gifted with a talent. Although often hidden, such talents are there for us to discover. God grants these gifts; they wait to be unveiled. The teens within whom these gifts hide call to us to help them discover the beauty within them; they await our invitation for them to lead and inspire us.

However, before we can see this great beauty within our teens, we must challenge our own stereotypes, prejudices and misconceptions. We must be willing to see them with new eyes, to hear them with new ears, and, in the process, to embrace the world with a new heart. "The Kingdom of God belongs to teenagers such as these," Jesus says. The challenge for us is to look and listen in ways that open us to their wisdom, their innocence and their simplicity of faith that will bring us closer to God's Kingdom.

3: Doreen's Story

Never in my wildest dreams did I imagine that I my work would be so enriching, inspiring and filled with God's love. I know that the teens I have counseled over the years have inspired me much more than I have inspired them. They live in an often cruel and unforgiving world, but in return they forgive and make this world better through their genuine love. Working with teenagers, I have learned that:

- No obstacle is too great—I have seen them overcome unbelievable obstacles.
- No mountain is too high—I have watched them climb them all.
- No dream is beyond reach—I have witnessed them achieving the biggest of dreams.

The obstacles confronting Doreen appeared insurmountable, but she turned them into challenges. It was as if I watched her climbing a series of high, steep mountains; each time I thought she was about to fall, she would find another rock to cling to.

Doreen's father abandoned the family when she was a baby. She was raised by her mother, a prostitute and an alcoholic. As a young teenager, Doreen fled this abusive home to live on the streets. Like so many young girls trapped in a world with so little opportunity and hope, she resorted to doing many things just to survive—things she later regretted.

I was amazed at Doreen's ability to forgive those who hurt her. She held no bitterness toward her parents, maintained a will to survive, and was determined to make something better of her life. By the grace of God and with the help of many people, Doreen turned her life around. She settled into a youth home for street kids, achieved an "A" average in school, and became a model student, an inspiration to other students in her school.

I had the pleasure of spending a lot of time with Doreen and grew to love her dearly. The more she allowed me into her heart, the more I noticed her enchanting inner beauty. Whenever Doreen entered my office, she filled it with energy, enthusiasm and a brilliant smile. She overflowed with love and life. I witnessed many of her talents over the years, especially her ability to work with younger kids who loved her because she was gentle and understanding.

Shortly after Doreen's graduation, she and I went out on the town to celebrate. We ate at a quiet restaurant and talked about everything, and, as usual, enjoyed each other's company. Just before it came time to leave, I asked her, "What are your dreams and hopes for the future?"

She answered quickly: "To attend college in September, to have a profession in child-care, and to have my own children some day." She then stared into the distance, looking over my shoulder. It was as if she was about to say something else, but hesitated.

"Is that all?" I asked. "Is there more?"

"Just one thing more. I want to marry a man who will treat me well and never hurt me."

I lowered my head for a moment to regain my composure; I did not want her to see the tears welling up in my eyes. After a few seconds I raised my head and asked her, "Will your dreams come true?"

"I believe the first three will," she said, "but the last one is unlikely."

Doreen's dreams for the future kept her climbing toward the summit, enabling her to cling to hope and greet each day with new excitement. She dreamed wonderful, yet simple dreams. These dreams gave her the strength to make it to the top of life's toughest peaks.

Teens don't ask for any more out of life than any of us expect—the opportunity to work, to be productive, to have loving relationships and to provide for their family. These simple dreams demonstrate just how pure, innocent, humble and selfless our teenagers are.

Doreen's inner beauty was there for us all to discover. She had so much to give in spite of how cruel life had been to her, despite how often she had been violated and hurt.

It was her simple dreams that kept her going, and so it is with teenagers—they ask for little from life and are willing to give a lot.

Thank you, Lord, for Doreen. I am sure she will give to many of your children the love she never knew. And I pray, Lord, that you make all of her dreams come true. Amen.

Quick Tips

- Never discount a teenager's dreams. Whether simple or complex, attainable or unattainable, dreams offer motivation and hope; nurture them.
- As much as possible, believe in the dreams of teens. Believing with them builds their self-confidence. Teens may gain more from your confidence in their ability than from attaining the specifics of their dreams.
- As you encourage teens to pursue their dreams, also challenge them to make the best of life, no matter how things turn out.

On Sharing Your Story

Teenagers will occasionally ask about our child-hood to discover more about us. They are looking for a window through which to understand who we *are*, rather than the roles we currently play as parents, teachers or leaders. They look for qualities in us that will help them shape their identity and cope with weakness. These are special opportunities for us to share with teens more about our hidden selves.

But be cautious! How often have you said to a teenager, "When I was your age..." and then launched into a detailed description of how difficult your life was, how much tougher you had to be, and how your parents were the world's strictest disciplinarians? Teens will think more highly of us if we paint true pictures of our lives as teens rather than inflated, fabricated ones. Avoid exaggerating the difficulties you went through to make yourself look more heroic. Avoid telling stories designed to make teens feel guilty about how good they have it or ashamed of the mistakes they make.

I can remember making this mistake with my own children. I shared with them on a number of occasions how poor we were when I was young. ("Poor us!") On other occasions I shared with them that whenever Easter, Christmas and birthdays arrived, the house was filled with gifts...in fact, entire *rooms* would be filled with gifts! ("How great we had it!")

Finally, curious, they challenged me, "Dad, how could you have been so poor and yet your parents filled your home with gifts?" They got me! And getting caught caused me to look back and reassess.

Although I know my parents sacrificed to provide for us—my father rode a bike to work instead of buying a car—we were not poor.

Being honest about your past, especially with its mistakes, gives teens an opportunity to realize that their own journey in life is much like yours. Share the stupid and funny things you did. Confess your foolishness. Tell about the time the time you drank too much and made a fool of yourself with that date you really had a crush on. Your teenagers will realize that you too had to learn from your mistakes. Most important, they will learn from you one of life's most treasured virtues: humility. Share your frailty and teens will laugh with you and discover the meaning of redemption.

Quick Tips

- **Speak honestly and openly to teens about your experiences. Share your human weaknesses and frailties. Teens will think more of you, not less, and gain confidence in their journey.**
- **Model gratitude for teenagers. Let go of the attitude that life owes you, or that you should feel guilty if life is going well. Stop complaining. Gratitude heals.**
- **Being a parent, teacher or leader does not elevate your status. You are not a superior being, just older and more experienced. Embrace your humanness; you will gain credibility in the eyes of teens.**
- **All of us—teenagers included—learn from life's experiences. Invite teens to share what they learn as they cope with life's challenges.**

4: Myths and Misconceptions

"Teenagers are disrespectful!" "Teenagers are loud!"
"Teenagers are self-centered!" "Teenagers are lazy!"

Sound familiar? Misconceptions about teenagers abound.
Viewed from the outside, occasionally running into them
on the street or in the mall, such conclusions may seem
warranted. But what we don't see is what matters—the
myths dissolve when we enter their hearts and souls.

Myth #1: Teenagers like everything loud.

Because teens occasionally play their music loudly, talk to
friends loudly and party loudly, we come to characterize
them as loud and expect them to be most comfortable when
the volume is cranked up.

Oddly enough, the opposite is true. Most teens prefer quiet
environments. Like all of us, they may at times drown out
their worries with music, television or laughter, but the loud-
ness of life can become an irritant for them as well.

The need for quiet is evident especially at home. For teens,
a quiet home represents safety, a badly needed refuge from a
hectic, confusing world.

In particular, teens don't want loud interactions with their
parents. They dislike it when parents shout, either as a
way to express anger or as a tool to discipline. Kids understand when they have stepped out of line or violated a house rule; they *expect* to be spoken to about it—and disciplined, if

necessary. However, they want this done as it is done in the adult world—quietly and respectfully. As adults, we expect the same treatment in the workplace—correction, communicated calmly and fairly.

For teens, the message is the same whether we scream it or say it quietly. Screaming, in fact, gets in the way of what we say. A stern, rational voice communicates well; a loud, emotional voice does not. Kids from loud homes experience higher levels of anxiety, find their homes uncomfortable and learn to communicate improperly. Teens from quiet homes experience less anxiety, feel safe at home and learn to communicate their anger and hurt in healthy ways.

Quick Tips

● Provide teens the quiet space they need to feel safe.
● Speak to teens in the same respectful, reasonable tone as you would expect from a co-worker, friend or supervisor.

Myth #2: Teenagers are vulgar and enjoy using vulgar language.

We occasionally hear teens use vulgar language and curse in public, either as name-calling or to be noticed. In reality, the majority of teens do not appreciate cursing, especially from adults. They find it unprofessional, immature and vulgar.

Why, if teenagers dislike vulgar language, do they occasionally use it? In large part because our world models it for them. They learn it from parents, relatives, the media, sometimes even teachers. Repeatedly hearing vulgarity eventually teaches teens that vulgarity is an acceptable form of communication, an easy, unthinking way to stir emotion and grab attention.

In all the years I have worked with teenagers, I have heard them use vulgar language only on rare occasions. I find vulgarity much more common in the adult world.

Quick Tip

● Don't use vulgar language with teens or in the presence of teens.

Myth #3: Teenagers are quick to judge others, gossip and spread rumors.

Only rarely will teenagers destroy friends through gossip. Most teens are quick to defend the weaker members of society. They judge rarely and are surprisingly forgiving toward a world that often treats them cruelly.

When I do hear teens judging others and gossiping about them, I typically ask, "What is the nature of the adult world in which they live?" Many of them come from homes where parents are quick to judge and name-call.

Kids are not as cruel as we think they are *because they know how much it hurts*. Teenagers are just beginning to come to a place of personal power and decision-making, taking the first steps toward determining their place in the world. To this point, they find themselves at the bottom rung of the cultural ladder, told what to do and when. They know from recent, firsthand experience what it means to be teased, rejected and overlooked. Their compassion—much greater than that often found in adults—flows from their immediate identification with those who struggle for acceptance.

Quick Tips

- Don't gossip, whether with teens or elsewhere.
- Encourage the expression of teenagers' natural empathy; invite them to identify with the outcast and marginalized.

Myth #4: Teenagers want nothing to do with their families.

God has given all teenagers a job: *obtain more freedom*. This is their developmental responsibility, a normal and healthy part of what drives them. This struggle to obtain more freedom may look, to the adults around them, like they want to be free of their families and do whatever they want without regard for the limits set by home and society. This is not the case. Teenagers love spending time with their families. They long to be close to them.

In their world, home offers the safest and most loving environment, a place of refuge.

Teens find themselves in a peculiar bind: parents and siblings—the very people from whom they seek freedom—are the people on whom they most rely. They seem to push against what they know they need—the family bond; they appear to reject what they desperately desire—a family that will always be there for them, a constant, reliable source of love.

What dynamic operates here? It is not *freedom* from parents, home and siblings that teens want, but greater *autonomy*. In many ways, the teenager actually depends more on the love and stability of a family than a child. By the time they are teens, they have experienced the harshness of the world, and come to understand that the one constant in their lives will be family. They may lose their jobs, friends may desert them —even their own family structure may break down—but they believe that their parents will always be there for them.

Do not be fooled by teenagers' desire to stay out later and more often. This does not mean they want to break from you; it means they are searching for their own place in life. Teenagers desire more autonomy when it comes to decisions concerning them. They expect more democracy when it comes to making decisions about family life. This freedom is not to be interpreted as freedom *from* you; it is more accurately freedom *with* you. They do not want to break from home and parents, they want the relationship redefined.

Quick Tips

● Read up on the stages of human development. Understand and discuss with other teachers, leaders and parents of youth the developmental tasks of teens.
● It's not freedom from authority that teens want, but greater autonomy.

Myth #5: Teenagers only want adults around to give them things and satisfy their needs.

Teens need you a lot more than you might believe. We might think otherwise, because they are constantly moving. They live busy and challenging lives as they struggle to find their way in an increasingly complex and difficult world. Your role in their lives—whether as teacher, parent, counselor, youth worker or family friend—takes on a new form as what they need from you shifts. They still *need* you, but in different ways.

Over the last couple of decades, we accepted the belief that kids do not necessarily need a lot of time with us, as long as the time we spend with them is "quality" time, time focused just on them, time when we are actively engaged with them.

Through my work, I have discovered something surprisingly different: while they appreciate the one-on-one time we share with them, what teens value most is *availability*. If teenagers had their way, the adults with whom they are in relationship would be available to them *always*, whether a parent at home, a trusted neighbor in the house down the block, a counselor in her office at school or a youth worker in his office at church. Kids want their families and adults *there* even though they may not interact with them all the time or even most of the time.

At home, for example, teens want to be able to turn to their parents throughout the evening to ask a question or share an idea. As unrealistic as it may sound, kids tell me that they want their parents home *even when the teens themselves are not home!* It gives them assurance and a sense of stability. If you are a parent, and an entire night passes with only ten or twenty words spoken between you and your teens, know that they feel comfort and security in knowing you are with them. A lot of communication occurs in the silence.

Quick Tip
- Being available for teenagers provides great security and comfort.

Myth #6: Teenagers do not want discipline.

Wrong. Teenagers *desire* discipline. How often I've heard these sad words: "If my parents really cared about me, they would set some rules and discipline me."

As a counselor, I know that kids—from young children to teenagers—neither respect nor appreciate parents who allow themselves to be manipulated and their kids to run wild. Kids respect and appreciate fair discipline that they helped shape. Interestingly, when teens are asked to discipline other teens for violating school rules, they will often recommend consequences more severe than those set by adults.

Truth is, most teens live lives more disciplined than those of adults! They work all day in school, participate in after-school sports or other activities, then do homework and their household chores. They have to be careful all the time with what they say and how they approach people. They live in a world where they are subject to adults, struggle to be accepted and work hard to appease friends and family. I consider this to be a challenging, demanding and disciplined life!

Kids want a home with fair rules and consistent discipline, rules and discipline that apply equally to everyone. This gives order to the homes and lives, and teaches them responsibility and respect for the rights of those to whom they relate and live.

When so much else is changing for teens—relationships, bodies, responsibilities—rules and discipline offer stability and demonstrate to them that they are loved and respected.

Quick Tips

- When it comes to discipline, teenagers want clear boundaries and consistent consequences.
- Rules offer stability in a constantly changing and chaotic world.

Myth #7: Teenagers are only interested in money and material possessions.

Teens are not interested in money or having parents with lots of money. The most beautiful kids I have ever met came from humble backgrounds. Their families never had much; their parents worked hard to make a living. Most important, the parents put their kids, not money, at the top of their priority list.

Most kids understand why working parents are gone so much of the time and appreciate what their parents do to help the family survive. They love their parents for the endless sacrifices they make to provide a decent life for their children. These kids do not need much in the way of material things because the love is enough.

But, most kids do *not* understand or appreciate it when parents are gone all the time to work *because they want more than what they need*. These kids know when parents cross the line from a humble but comfortable lifestyle to materialism and greed. They do not believe their parents when they say, "I am doing this for you."

The kids know when parents lie to them, when what the parents really mean is, "I'm doing this for me." Kids resent parents who neglect them for the sake of making more money. The extras are never worth cheating kids of our time and energy. Money is never as important to kids as love, time together and a happy home.

But what of those teens for whom money seems to be a top priority? We visit this issue in Chapter 10.

Quick Tip

● Teenagers value adult availability over money or "things."

Myth #8: Teenagers are primarily influenced by their peers.

When I hear people talk about teenagers, I usually hear them complain about "peer pressure." The influence of peer pressure on teens seems to be legendary, but is it really as pervasive as adults imagine? In actuality, the influence of peers pales in comparison to the influence of, first, a loving and caring home, and second, television and the media.

Teenagers know that their teenage friends are still kids—just like them. Teenagers turn to peers because they are the ones who most closely share their experiences, who best understand them, just as adults turn to friends and associates for the same reasons. But teens believe that adults speak with knowledge and life experience that they have not yet acquired. They look to parents and adult friends to provide a stable, consistent, healthy perspective on life and decision-making. Peer influence gains power when the home does not provide the guidance, love and understanding that teenagers need.

Quick Tips

● Recognize the value of peers; teenagers' friends provide understanding, strength and loyalty during difficult times.
● A strong, loving home minimizes the results of peer pressure.

Myth #9: Teenagers are not interested in religion, faith or spiritual things.

I frequently hear this complaint, and I realize where it comes from: Religion often turns teenagers off, especially when forced upon them or used to foster shame or quilt.

Teens are turned on, however, by spirituality, faith, love for neighbor and God's love for them. Go into any school and tell the kids about people in need, people asking for their help, and the teens will overwhelm you with their response:

• Collect toys at Christmas or food at Thanksgiving, and teens will give whatever is needed.

• Talk with them about how much God loves them and that God values them as special children, and their eyes will light up with recognition and acceptance.

• Organize relevant, involving, purposeful prayer services, and they will express their faith in both God and the Church.

Scholars theorize that most of the apostles were only teenagers when recruited by Jesus. He forced nothing on these young people—he simply invited them. When they felt his love, they responded zealously. Given the chance, teenagers will surprise and perhaps even shock you with the depth of their spirituality. Reach out to them, take the risk, and invite them to lead you on their (and your) spiritual journey; you will be made holier from the path you walk together. Invite them to minister and bless you, and you will be astounded by how much closer to God you feel.

In the next chapter, I share the story of Bruno. Bruno's story demonstrates how misled we can be about the great love and spirituality that exists within even the roughest teens. Bruno shows how tough, wayward kids, when given the opportunity, can shine as beacons of Christ's love.

We can let go of these myths and misconceptions about teenagers. Most teens find distasteful the very things for which we criticize them: violence, vulgarity, materialism, promiscuity and secularism. When most in touch with themselves, they choose the higher ground.

Quick Tips

- Offer teens practical opportunities to respond in compassion and love to those in need.
- Be an example; the most powerful catalyst for revealing a teen's inner spiritual life will be your willingness to develop and reveal your own.
- Talk about God's love. Invite teens, honestly and gently, to lead you in furthering your own spiritual journey.

5: Bruno's Story

Early on the third day of school, just before classes started, my phone rang. I heard the anxious voice of a mother: "My son is so frightened of school that he won't come out of the house. Will you see him?"

"First tell me why he refuses to go to school."

She explained that in the first couple of days of school there were a number of kids who were "initiated." Initiation took many forms: shaving kids' heads, shoving kids' heads into toilets, forcing kids to push pennies on the floor with their noses. The boy was so frightened he would be targeted, that he would not go to school.

I agreed to meet with the boy.

An hour passed before I heard a knock at my door. The mother appeared with her timid young son. He stood about 4'11" and could not have weighed more then 90 pounds. I understood why he was afraid. In addition, he had a very gentle face, soft skin and a shy look. The glasses didn't help. I asked them into my office. Reluctantly, he entered. His name was Trevor.

It only took a few seconds of conversation before Trevor's eyes welled up with tears and he started to sob. The more I tried to calm him, the more he cried. The more I tried to reassure him that his fears were unrealistic, the more frightened he became. My heart went out to him. I personally had never experienced such fear in school as a teenager, but could feel, to some extent, the anxiety he felt.

As Trevor continued crying, his mother softly told me that Trevor had no father nor siblings. What I believe she was telling me was that Trevor had no male role model, no one to teach him how to handle such difficult situations.

The more I spoke to Trevor, the more he cried. Every time I tried to make the situation better, it got worse. He soon became so frightened that I didn't know if I would get him out of my office. "I'm never coming back to school," he sobbed. He didn't care if the police came to get him, he was *not* going to return to school. Trevor's mother grew increasingly frantic. He continued crying. I sat back, stymied.

We sat this way for a minute before I said to Trevor, "I am going to leave my office for a few minutes. When I return, I'm bringing the roughest, toughest, meanest, most vicious kid in this school. I will return with a kid so tough he could bite the head off a lion. He plays on the senior football team and he has a reputation for being mean."

Trevor's crying turned to a more gentle sob. He raised his head and gave me an inquisitive look. I continued, "And then, Trevor, I am going to get this mean, tough kid to be your buddy. He will protect you and watch over you. If I do this will you then return to class?"

Trevor stopped sobbing, paused for a moment, then nodded his head yes. His tense posture started to relax.

Though it was obvious Trevor felt some relief, I did not. I was taking a chance. I made a promise and didn't know if I could deliver. I pulled the class schedule from my desk and scanned it for Bruno's name. No one messed with Bruno. Even I feared to approach him. I left my office and went to retrieve my messiah.

I stand six feet tall, and I have to look up at Bruno when I speak to him. He is four inches taller then me and twice as wide, with a stern face complementing his physical stature —in a word, intimidating. "Bruno," I began, "I need your help." I explained the situation. I asked, simply, if he would be Trevor's friend and take care of the boy. I held my breath.

Sober, serious, Bruno generously responded, "Sure I would, sir." I breathed again. Off to my office we went.

Upon arriving in my office, I introduced Bruno to Trevor. Initially, Bruno's size and presence immobilized Trevor; he could not even get off the couch to shake Bruno's hand. Bruno immediately moved toward Trevor, reached down, shook his hand and then sat beside him. "Now tell me," Bruno said to Trevor, "who has hurt you? I'll fix them so they never hurt you again."

I jumped in: "No, Bruno, nobody hurt Trevor! What we need is for you to look after him." Bruno may have been itching for a good fight.

As Trevor and Bruno talked, slowly becoming comfortable with each other, I watched Bruno, the large, tough,

street-fighter, turn into a gentle lamb, genuinely moved by Trevor's fear and sincerely wanting to help him. "You'll be all right," Bruno assured him. As Bruno grew more gentle, Trevor grew bolder; as Bruno settled back into the couch, Trevor sat further forward, straighter, shoving his chest out into the air; as Bruno spoke more softly, Trevor spoke more loudly. I could see Trevor's confidence building.

I smiled as the two of them left together, seventeen inches and more than a hundred pounds separating them. Side by side they walked. Trevor's mother and I knew that things would work out fine.

Even though we were once teenagers, it is difficult for most of us to recall and feel again the fears and anxieties we experienced at the time. Trevor's fear was real and justified. We must acknowledge and treat it as legitimate. The fact that we may never have experienced that fear ourselves does not mean it does not or cannot exist. The feelings of teenagers are not exaggerated or dramatized, they are real to them and they can be crippling. We have to treat them and their feelings as legitimately as we treat our own.

With teenagers like Bruno we are often too quick to judge. We draw conclusions about them based on the way they look, their size, demeanor and sometimes deviant behavior. But it is often the Brunos that turn out to be the most generous and helpful, the most sensitive and compassionate. They only need a little direction, an expressed belief in them and the opportunity and challenge to do great things. As adult leaders and parents, we empower them by giving them the opportunity. Look to them for leadership. Like St. Paul—who as Saul was an obnoxious persecutor—the Brunos will sometimes be the greatest converts, lifting all of us to new heights.

Bruno is not an isolated case; I have worked with many Brunos over the years, always astounded by what I see happen in the lives of problem kids when they are given the responsibility and autonomy to accomplish important tasks. If we rid ourselves of the misconceptions and myths, and look past the rough external surface, we discover within surprising potential and beauty. If we believe in them more than they believe in themselves, amazing things happen. Like St. Peter—another unexpected New Testament "gem" —Bruno was rough on the outside and sometimes quick to temper, but hid within energy and compassion just waiting for the chance to serve, heal and transform.

Lord, just as you called your apostle Paul centuries ago, today you call all of us to a life of love, peace and service. Send your Spirit to relieve our fear. Open our eyes to the many ways we can be your hands and feet, voice and eyes of compassion. Amen.

Quick Tips

- Teens' frustrations and anxieties are as real to them as ours are to us. Acknowledge this reality.
- If given the opportunity, even the roughest kids can be transformed and show their greatness.
- Teens love to make a difference in the lives of others. They appreciate it when you ask them to help and feel honored when you entrust them with challenging tasks.
- When a teen asks for help, pay close attention as you offer suggestions. A small response may indicate you are helping. Pursue it!
- Make use of this powerful, influential tool: teens ministering to teens.

On Communication

Whether at home, at school or in the parish, communicate well and you lay the groundwork for healthy relationships.

Who communicates better, adults or teens? My vote? The teens! While I find many adults to be guarded and suspicious, teens tend to wear their hearts on their sleeves, allowing quick insight into their emotions. They share their deepest thoughts willingly when they know an adult cares and will listen.

Quick Tips

- Screaming matches silence kids and inhibit communication.
- A relaxed atmosphere fosters communication. So does a gentle voice.
- Do not threaten. Do not ask threatening questions. Do not use words or gestures that threaten teens.
- Do not judge what teens say; listen to gain understanding.

Teens disagreeing with adults are not necessarily expressing disrespect. They are thinking for themselves—an appropriate developmental task at this age; be thankful that they are beginning to make their own way in life. You do not have to agree with their point of view, but please welcome and respect it.

What of the teens who resort to yelling to try to make their points? Or those who withdraw into sullen silence? I often see these methods of communicating (or not communicating) modeled for these teens at home. It is not their natural way. Teenagers are sincere, honest, genuine and sensitive people—prime candidates for insightful, warm communication. Provide the safe setting, open yourself up, and see what you can learn.

Quick Tips

- If you disagree with things teens say, present your views, with conviction, from your own experience. Your purpose is not to change the teens, but to be in dialogue. You can challenge them, gently, with questions.
- Do not undermine what teenagers think or feel. Do not discount their perceptions.
- Summarize what teens tell you; ask if you have understood.
- Work toward compromise, but always value respect and love over comfortable resolution.

6: Hidden Talents

Many parents come to my office upset because their children do poorly in school. These parents have tried everything—positive reinforcement, working closely with teachers, testing, tutoring. For many of their kids, nothing seems to help; the kids continue to do poorly in their studies, and their parents become increasingly distraught, ready to give up, frustrated and hurt.

In most cases, the parents have accepted the theory that in order to have a successful, stable, happy life, you must do well in school. They believe that only if you excel academically will you have a chance in the "real world." "If you can't cut it in school," they say, "then you face a bleak future."

The first thing I do with these parents is tell them the story of Jerry:

There was a young man named Jerry who read and wrote poorly and failed at whatever he tried at school. He stuck with it as long as he could, and then, when he could no longer stand the rejection and failure, he quit and left for the working world.

In his first job, Jerry cleaned outhouses in a public park. He loved his job. He worked outside, got lots of exercise and took great pride in what he did. At the end of his first month, his boss asked him to fill out an inventory sheet; Jerry had to complete orders for toilet paper, chemicals and other cleaning materials. But Jerry could not fill out the forms. He lost the job.

Jerry then got a job on the assembly line at a car company. He loved this job as well. Every night he went home tired and hungry, feeling good about what he had accomplished. At the end of the first month he was asked to fill out a another form. The form required him to log the number of cars completed and the time it took, along with calculating the time it took per car. He also had to order the necessary amount of replacement parts. Once again, Jerry could not fill out the form. And once again, he was dismissed.

It finally dawned on Jerry that he had to get into an area of work that did not require reading, writing or mathematical calculations. Jerry gave it some thought, then decided to take what little money he had and buy a gas lawn mower and grass trimmer. He knocked on doors, asking people if they wanted their grass cut. He did such a good job of mowing lawns—taking great pride in his work—that he ended up with more customers then he could handle. He hired other workers. He set up a company. Jerry's smartest decision? He hired an accountant to handle the paperwork. His company grew so large, and he made so much money, that he started investing in other areas. Within ten years, Jerry was a multimillionaire, with stores, restaurants, taxi cabs—and, of course, a landscaping company. Instead of one accountant, now a whole a team of lawyers and accountants took care of the paperwork.

One day his bank manager phoned him and asked him if he would be willing to loan a young local businessman some money. It was a risky venture, and the bank was not willing to take the chance. They thought of Jerry because of his reputation as an entrepreneur. Was he willing to take the chance and lend the money?

Jerry went to the bank, listened to the business proposition from the manager, and decided he would invest in this young man. The manager put together all the paperwork and asked Jerry to sign. Jerry took the pen and made an X where his signature was to go.

The bank manager looked at the signature and then said to Jerry, "What is this?"

"That's my signature."

The bank manager chuckled and said, "Jerry, you have to write your name."

Jerry replied, "I cannot read or write."

Astonished, the bank manager sat back in his chair. "You can't read or write! You have amassed millions of dollars and you can't read or write. I would have liked to see what you would have accomplished if you could read and write."

Jerry quickly responded, "If I could read and write, I'd be cleaning outhouses."

Every time I tell this story, parents feel more at ease with their own kids' failures with school. I believe they quickly recall—as you may be doing as you read this—all the friends and associates they have known through the years who, despite dropping out of school and experiencing early failures in life, ended up successful and happy.

Quick Tips

- Don't measure success by school performance. Teenagers are gifted and talented, often in areas that stretch beyond school. Help them find these gifts.
- Help teens value their gifts, no matter where they show up.

The point is, we all have gifts and talents, most of which show up in areas of life outside of school. Gifts such as artistic brilliance, work ethic, creative thinking, personality, personal skills, entrepreneurship, communication skills, intuition, instinct, spiritual development, emotional and psychological development, maturity, prudence, wisdom, fortitude—all are also critical life skills and qualities, yet seldom the focus of the classroom.

Never assume that our teenagers are failures because they do not fit into the molds society creates for them. Instead, encourage uniqueness and creativity...encourage them to succeed *in life*. Let them dream their dreams. Urge them to follow those dreams, and assure them that you are with them on the journey. Pick them up when they fall. In short, *believe in them*. Believing in our teens inspires them to believe in themselves.

Then no mountain is too large to climb, no obstacle too great to conquer, no dream too impossible to make real, no failure too great to accept. In fact, if we believe in our teenagers, their failures will no longer be failures, but life experiences that bring them to greater maturity.

This is success, not measured in dollars, but in fulfillment. We succeed in life when we accept our limitations, realize our gifts, do what we love and serve the world.

I spoke to a parent once who had given up on his daughter, concluding that she would never amount to anything. He dismissed as useless the only talent the girl displayed—cooking.

I pointed out to him that his daughter's ability in the kitchen could make her a millionaire some day. I told him about a local caterer, a woman who had immigrated from another country and, after years of cooking for family and friends, eventually opened her own catering business. She had no formal education and could not speak English. Her "hidden talent" is now worth millions, and she owns one of the most prestigious banquet halls in our city.

Such greatness comes from within! It is there in our teens, ready to be unleashed. We can be the catalyst that helps them discover these latent treasures, talents and gifts.

In the next chapter I share my experience with Mike, whose great talent lay hidden, buried underneath layers of insecurity and fear. The educational system and society's standards labeled Mike a failure. He faced a bleak future. Little did we realize how brilliantly Mike could shine.

Quick Tips

- Let up on the pressure to succeed academically. Teens already feel this far more than we realize.
- Let teens live *their* dreams, not yours.

7: Mike's Story

I have taught and counseled teenagers for over two decades. In all that time, every teen I have ever met has been gifted in some unique way. *Every one of them.* Each and every teenager has a gift to offer the world.

I remember Mike. I taught him in a grade 10 theology class. Other teachers described him as "a nice boy, but weak academically." Mike scored poorly on tests and assignments. "Learning disabilities," they said, in a tone that held little promise for Mike's future.

I gave Mike's theology class a challenging assignment. They had to write a two-thousand word essay on a topic of their own choosing, provided it dealt with a moral issue and involved some theological or philosophical dimension. I required footnotes and a bibliography, with no restrictions on the amount of research to be done. I left the assignment fairly open-ended, allowing lots of room for students to demonstrate their strengths and to stay within their comfort levels.

Of all the papers I read, Mike's caught my attention. He chose as his topic "War: Just or Unjust." He did some research, but mostly chose to explore his own thought and opinion. His finished essay brilliantly interwove fact and theory—magnificent! He cut to the heart of a complex issue from a number of perspectives—theological, practical, economical and philosophical. He even included some beautiful poetry.

I wondered if the essay was truly Mike's.

I asked Mike to stay after the next class. He stood beside me at my desk. These moments are always difficult for me; I challenged him: "Mike, is this really your work?"

Mike immediately assured me that he had indeed written the essay. "It's my work!" he insisted.

I tried another tack, discussing the essay with him. He quickly convinced me: he demonstrated not only a clear grasp of the content, but talked of other, related issues with ease. I also discovered Mike's passion for writing short stories and poetry. I found this absolutely amazing. Why had Mike's interests and gifts not come to light in any of his other classes or assignments, especially English?

"No one knows about my writing," Mike said. "Not even my parents. I write at night when everyone in the house is asleep."

"Mike," I asked, "would you bring in some of your work for me to read?"

A few days later Mike came to class hauling an oversized duffel bag. After class, he brought the bag to my desk and began pulling out four-inch thick binders, one after another, each binder filled with pages...*thousands* of pages...of his writing...all *kinds* of writing. I felt overwhelmed by the sheer volume of it and stared at Mike in amazement. He seemed to be both reluctant and proud to share this product of his secret passion.

I spent the next few evenings reading Mike's work. I then brought it to the

English teachers and the Head of the English Department. Although they hesitated to admit that Mike's work was the product of a genius, they did admit their surprise. At my request they enrolled Mike in a university creative writing class. Throughout the following school year, Mike continued to struggle with his high school courses, but flourished in his university course.

Amazing gifts like Mike's lie hidden within every teenager, often undiscovered because the teens are timid or shy, or because no one gives them the opportunity to show their gifts to others. Some live unaware of their gifts.

To release these gifts, we need to go beyond the boundaries and limitations set by schools, families and society; we need to find creative, unconventional ways to help kids identify and experiment with their gifts. We have to boost their confidence and courage so they trust that they have something worth sharing.

Courage and confidence—there are many ways to develop these virtues in teens. One way is to challenge them to teach *us*. We can ask them their opinions on current issues as well as problems and dilemmas that we face. We can let them know that we make decisions with their input. Invite them to contribute in directing the life of the family (if you are a parent) or the focus of a class (if you are a teacher or youth worker). At times we will be amazed by the depth of their wisdom and prudence. We will quickly recognize their gifts.

I have met hundreds of teenagers who, like Mike, were brilliantly gifted. The structures of our educational systems and the restrictions of the adult world seldom provide an environment that allows these gifts to shine. We will not free our teens to shine by filling their minds with the knowledge we have acquired, rather, we have to approach every teenager with the awareness and conviction that there is within this child something grand to be discovered and unleashed. We have to listen, to observe, to affirm, to accept, to support, to love, to nurture—to hold up the lens through which their brightness can be focused and shared.

Lord, grant us—parents and educators—the patience and insight we need to see below the surface to discover the brilliant gifts you have given your teenage children. Amen.

Quick Tips

- Use unconventional methods to discover the hidden talent of a teenager—arts, sports, hobbies, music...whatever you can imagine. Reach beyond the classroom and the curriculum.
- Nurture teens' natural talents. Give them the autonomy to express them.
- Be willing to take risks to discover teens' hidden greatness.

On Phones and Chat Rooms

Is the use of the phone or on-line computer time causing stress for the teens and families in your life? I have a suggestion: add a phone line, just for them. An expensive solution? Maybe not.

The number one social tool for kids today is the phone. The use of the Internet is slowly closing the gap. Outside of school, homework, extracurricular activities, church responsibilities and home chores, teens enjoy little free time for socializing. The phone, and to some extent, the Internet, allow kids to talk with friends, discuss school business, get homework done and plan their weekends. With my teens I always think, Better they stay home talking on the phone than out on the streets; better they interact on-line than watch some mindless TV show; better they talk on the phone than walk around the house bored and restless. So about that extra phone line? In terms of convenience and cost of other entertainment options, it may be a great investment...and cheaper, too.

Within the last few years, Internet use has become a necessity for students. They do research, keep in touch with friends and travel the world. Though we object to the presence of pornography and other unhealthy content, the Internet provides a useful, enriching and increasingly necessary technological tool. As our Internet literacy grows, our ability to control the content that reaches our homes and schools also grows.

Our concern with the phone, the computer and the Internet is that our teens do not become obsessed with and controlled by them. Do not let these tools become another escape from the real world, the real self or real relationships, but rather, encourage their use as another avenue for authentic connection.

Quick Tips

- Consider adding another phone line if phone and on-line use becomes a source of conflict at home.
- Recognize the value of phone- and Internet-supported relationships.
- If you have a computer, a modem and Internet access in your home, become Internet literate; learn what is and is not available for teens and encourage the healthy use of Internet resources.

8: Insecurity
Uncovering Insecurity

Insecurity cripples, and its effects last a lifetime. Insecurity encourages kids to go along with the crowd, join gangs, be swayed by the powerful, do poorly in school and take risks with relationships. Insecurity allows teens to be used, abused and hurt. It keeps them from trusting themselves, feeling content and finding fulfillment and happiness.

Some kids display obvious signs of insecurity; they appear helpless and indecisive, easily intimidated, never assertive. They discount their abilities and retreat when challenged.

For many kids, however, the signs of insecurity are subtle and deceptive. This unsuspected insecurity shows itself in the kids who:
- appear confident and aggressive
- do well in school
- have lots of friends
- are popular
- lead
- look to be in control and happy

There is an uneasy falseness to these accomplishments *when kids achieve them because of their insecurity*. The insecurity motivates them to compensate for their true feelings, to cover the way they really see themselves. If such insecurity-motivated accomplishments really resulted in internal security and happiness, it would be a good thing, but most often, our teens do all these things only to discover that they did not rid themselves of the insecurity and unhappiness. There lies the danger.

Emotional upheaval frequently follows—fear, jealousy, suspicion, guilt, anger, regret, resentment, hatred of oneself and others. These emotions find expression as aggression directed either toward the outside world (e.g., cruelty or criminal behavior) or toward the self (e.g., laziness, apathy, drug abuse or attempted suicide). And we stand helplessly by, bewildered because we had interpreted their outward behavior as confidence, positive self-image and stability.

How can we discover these teens' true feelings before it is too late? We can ask, and we can listen: kids who suffer from insecurity are the first to admit that they feel useless, unworthy and incapable, despite impressive outward accomplishments. Simple questions yield honest, telling answers:

- How do you really feel about yourself?
- How are things going with you? How's your life these days?
- On a scale of 1 to 10, do you feel more like a 1 "completely insecure and unsure of myself"—or a 10—"totally secure and happy with who I am"?
- When it comes to your life, do you feel more like a "winner" or a "loser"?
- What do you like most about yourself? Name your biggest contributions to your family (school, friendships, church, etc.).

The media, the school, the family and the church all share the responsibility for creating feelings of insecurity in our kids. We spend too much time talking about perfection and pointing out failures. We obsess about "measuring" everyone and everything against unrealistic ideals. We focus on our *own* agendas, whether it be curriculum in school or our personal values. We spend too much time looking at the distance between what has been done and what could have been done. We are forever correcting wrongs. We look to reward the perfect performance that never comes.

We easily understand how children raised in a home where there is addiction, neglect, abuse or abandonment will likely grow to feel insecure, believing that they are unlovable or not worthy of love. But kids will similarly struggle with insecurity if they are raised in a home where the standards are set too high, where they have to measure up to be accepted and loved.

More to the point: we falsely believe that we achieve excellence by *eliminating* human weakness and frailty, when the truth is, excellence comes through *accepting and embracing* our humanity.

Quick Tips

● Insecurity reveals itself through relationship, not necessarily through successes or failures. Keep communication open and inviting.

● Expect no more from a teen in a given situation than you would from yourself.

● Create opportunities for teens to discover their passions, and through their passions, their gifts.

Schools and Insecurity

I believe that our educational system creates insecurity. It measures us against perfection, which we can never achieve. In addition, it *ranks* us, indicating what kind of person we are (advanced? general? basic? deficient?). Imagine being labeled a "basic" person. Imagine spending forty long, committed hours on a project—in essence, fully giving yourself to it—and then hearing that you had only achieved 60% of what was expected. Outrageous! The system chips away at your self-esteem. It says to you that no matter how hard you work you are only worth 60%—you are only three-fifths of a person!

Or imagine hearing from a teacher—and this happens often—"If you don't pass my subject, you won't get into college, and if you don't get to college, you seriously jeopardize your future." Ridiculous! Our worth and the outcome of our lives do not depend on how we perform in school.

Conversely, how we perform in school does not predict how we will perform in life. It is neither the secret for success nor a reflection of our value as people.

I often hear from parents and teachers, "I am not as concerned about the marks my children (or students) get as long as they try their hardest." The intention is to make the teens feel better, but such statements bring unexpected and problematic consequences:

- First, no matter how hard we try in life, we know we can always *try harder*. How hard is hard enough? Receiving this "assurance" feels far from assuring: we *know* we can always try harder, so we instinctively believe that we have not done enough—we have failed once again! Think of your own experience as an adult: no matter what you accomplish in life, you can always look back and imagine how you could have done a better job. But maturity comes from knowing when you have "done enough," when you have done the job, and it's a fine job, and striving for a perfect job is futile and a waste of your time and effort. My recommendation for our teens? Try this healthier option: say to them, "All I expect is a good and honest effort."
- Second, why should our teenagers work "their hardest" at tasks in which they have no interest or investment? If our teens do not like school—and most do not—why not "do enough" to meet the requirements, saving their energy for the things for which they have the greatest passion? How often in our lives do we, as adults, "try our hardest" at what we do? Don't we often—sensibly, intelligently— do as much as we have to to finish

the job? It is much healthier for Brian, who absolutely hates school and scores 70%, to be praised for achieving the 70%, and then encouraged to put his remaining energies into the areas he loves, the areas in which he will achieve greatness.

All institutions, including schools, are necessarily limited in their ability to span the scope of human experience. Our children's potential reaches far beyond any curriculum or program. A definition of "success" that places importance on power, status or money, lessens the possibility of nurturing teens whose gifts might lead to compassion, peace, self-expression and love—a very different view of "success." I suspect that God's definition of success leans toward the latter.

Can we open our eyes to the surprising gifts, talents and beauty of our teenagers? Can we rid ourselves of our narrow concepts of success? Can we respect and admire them for their very existence, not for "measuring up" to some arbitrary view of perfection? Can we embrace the idea that our teens will experience their greatest victories through their greatest flaws and weaknesses? Can our education system do all of this, increasing the likelihood of producing a population of secure people? Yes, but not without a great deal of hard work:

- revamping curriculum to acknowledge both the diversity of teenage gifts and the spectrum of human life-skills;
- letting go of methods of evaluation that pit kids against each other and against "perfection";

- accepting the limitations of formal education;
- maturing enough to understand that we often find the beauty of creation in the imperfect, the weak and the flawed.

Quick Tips

- Avoid saying, "Try your best." Instead say, "All I expect is a good, honest effort."
- Avoid focusing on grades and percentage points; look for measures of success that match teens' gifts. Better to discover or develop a natural gift than raise a grade a point.
- Initiate discussions with simple, honest questions.

Overcoming Insecurity

How do we move teens from insecurity to security? Here are a few ideas:

First, we can help free teenagers (and ourselves) from the unrealistic standards set up by school and society, and instead accept them (and ourselves) as miracles and gifts. Start by discussing with the teens in your home or classroom both the pluses and the minuses of school as they experience it. Let them share their frustrations with grading and ranking, with the narrowness of school offerings and their desire to invest themselves in areas of interest outside of school.

Acknowledge that their feelings are legitimate and healthy, and together talk about ways to "meet the requirement" of school, while still taking care of themselves and feeding their passions. Then repeat the same discussion, replacing "school" with "society," "church" and "family."

Second, allow teens the opportunities to discover and explore areas of personal interest. Listen more closely in conversations with them or as they speak with friends:

- Where do you hear enthusiasm and eagerness? What are they talking about at those times?
- How can those areas of interest be further examined? What other areas of school, church or community life might connect to this interest?
- Do you know of possible adult "mentors" who could help teens develop these special interests?

Third, help teens erase old, unhealthy tapes, those inner "recordings" that guide our perceptions and response to ourselves and the world. If it took a decade or two for teens to record the old tapes—"I'm not worth much; no matter what I do, it's not good enough"—it will take a long time to replace them with new, realistic tapes—"I have great talent; I am beautiful within; I'm incredibly valuable to God, myself and others." RE-recording those tapes happens as kids talk about and recognize that the source of their insecurity exists outside of them, in what they have been taught in an unhealthy home or by the false opinions of others (who, fortunately, are usually those the teens love most in life). It also happens as we honestly, openly identify the beauty we see within them and invite them to start articulating aloud the truth about themselves as you and God can see it.

Too often I have seen the greatness within teenagers buried under a blanket of insecurity. Living in fear and pain, they sit immobilized at the current time and threatened by the approaching demands of adulthood. And as adults, believing they are unworthy of love, they will pass this destructive belief to their own children or the children with whom they work. Our challenge? To transform our understanding of success, to dispel the myths about the importance of certain institutions and lifestyles, and to keep our eyes open to recognize and deal with insecurity in the teens in our lives.

In the next chapter I share the story of Sharon, struggling to overcome the insecurity caused by her abusive background.

9: Sharon's Story

"Her name is Sharon," the art teacher said, "and I want you to see her. I think she's depressed. She's been losing weight. And then there's the art she creates..." She paused before continuing: "It's disturbing. I've counseled her a little: she's a young girl with an ugly past, and she's having difficulty dealing with it."

The following day she brought Sharon to my office. I felt immediate concern: Sharon looked much too thin and very depressed. With the art teacher seated on one side of me and Sharon on the other, we began. I did not want to spend much time on trivial questions, so I attempted to get to the heart of the matter, asking her about her family, parents and siblings. Her parents were divorced. A court order prevented her father from contact with her and her siblings under age 16. We discussed at greater length her home life, both good experiences and bad.

When I touched on sensitive areas, Sharon turned cold, stared at the wall and fidgeted, rubbing her hands together and pulling at the ends of her thread-bare sweater sleeves. At times she pulled the sleeves down and completely hid her hands within them. Occasionally I reached forward slowly and touched her sleeve-covered hand. Each time, she tensed even more. In spite of that, I continued to touch her hand.

By the end of the session, I suspected that Sharon had experienced a number of traumatic life experiences, including

both neglect and sexual abuse. I found support for these conclusions in her artwork: Sharon consistently represented a
little girl playing with toys or walking in the park; off in the
distant sky appeared the face of a raging, hateful monster,
menacingly watching the little girl. The monster poised
ready to attack. Harsh, cold purples, blues and oranges sur-
rounded and ran through the monster's face. I also wondered
about an eating disorder, evidenced by Sharon's skeletal
frame. I observed her withdrawn posture and lack of respon-
siveness, and her overall negative view of herself. Sharon
showed a high level of insecurity and very low self-esteem.

After this first session, I asked her art teacher how she felt it
went. "I thought it went well," she said. "But..."

"But what?" I asked.

"I don't think you should have kept touching her. It made
her too uncomfortable. You especially crossed the line when
you hugged her as you left your office."

Had I? I tried to explain: "I suspect Sharon is the victim of a
long-lasting incestuous relationship. Being a male puts me at
a disadvantage—it's tougher to convince her that I really do
care for her, and that when I touch her, it's a touch of love.
I want her to know that she has nothing to fear from me
and that she can trust me. When she becomes convinced
of this, she won't fear me. Only then will she be okay
about sharing her past."

No matter the person or the problem—when I sense their anxiety, I
use touch to acknowledge the pain

and offer comfort. Most leave my office with a hug; I know of nothing more therapeutic and healing. Hugs do so much, conveying hard-to-articulate emotions, giving energy, bonding people, transferring the heat and warmth of love, communicating that my office is a place of care and safety. Most important, it establishes the kind of relationship that brings the teen back for another session.

In general, boys are more reluctant to hug, a sad result of cultural bias. With some of them, therefore, I offer a firm double handshake. Male or female, I handle each situation differently according to the comfort level of the teen. At the same time, sometimes pushing the cultural boundaries opens up new opportunities for growth. In many situations, those who react most negatively to touch and hugs are the ones that have never received healthy hugs or were violated in some way. These most need such touch—healthy, warm, comforting, safe, healing.

Quick Tips

- Demonstrate that teens can feel safe with you. Listen non-judgmentally; keep their secrets; be trustworthy.
- Be patient. It may take a while before trust develops and teens open up and share their stories.

Sharon and I made slow progress; I remember the pain of session after session ending with Sharon still unable to tell "her story." Insecure about everything, she could not believe she had anything of value to offer the world. She felt unworthy of the treasures the world had to offer her. Would she ever be able to talk about her past? Only when she believed she could trust me.

Hope dawned when I realized that, at the end of each session, Sharon waited for my hug...even though she stood in tree-like rigidity with her arms by her side. Still, she *wanted* to be hugged! In subsequent sessions, the hugs became stronger and longer. Eventually, her arms made their way around my back. I remember the first time I actually felt her hands on my back—a breakthrough. Sharon needed to be hugged. But she also needed to know that I would never hurt her, that she was with someone who only cared for her and wanted to make her whole again.

Slowly, too, Sharon began to reveal her incestuous past, including years of abuse by an uncle and her father. She had also attempted suicide. But the more she shared, the less anxious she felt; the more she talked about what had been done to her, the less it imprisoned her; the more she acknowledged the possibility of her own inner beauty, the more she revealed herself as a wonderful, talented, beautiful child of God. She put on weight and regained her physical health. She continued to develop as an artist, demonstrating brilliant talent. Once freed of the stifling anxiety and the constant preoccupation with covering her scarred wrists, Sharon blossomed.

How dare any human being violate a child's dignity the way Sharon's had been violated! I still feel the anger I felt when counseling her. What do you say to teenagers like Sharon who have been abused so horribly?

"The people who did this to you are cruel and ill."

"Even though this was done to you, you are an innocent and beautiful child of God."

"God calls you to arise from the darkness and see the great beauty that exists within you—the same beauty I see right now."

Lord, I pray that Sharon and all your children who have been broken by this kind of abuse be healed again by your love and warmth, so they can feel secure and see the greatness within themselves. Amen.

Quick Tips

● Abused kids need to know it was never their fault. They were the victims of another person's illness.

● Pushing cultural boundaries can open new opportunities for growth.

On Friendships

Many of the kids who come to me for counseling bring their friends with them to the sessions. They do this because they need their friends' love and support. Even when they get comfortable with me, some continue to bring their friends. The friends do not have to say anything—just their presence gives assurance.

The degree to which friends minister to each other indicates the strength of the friendship, and, on that basis, I have witnessed some *amazing* friendships! In many ways teens do it better than adults, approaching their ministry to each other with great innocence and sincerity.

The worst has happened at our school a number of times: *a student dies.* In these horrific circumstances I watch kids powerfully minister to each other, giving strength, knowing exactly what to say and when to say it. I sit back and watch them work their healing with each other.

Be careful about evaluating the friends of the teenagers you know and love. It might help to spend a moment thinking about *your* friends: they may appear normal to you, but looking at them through the eyes of those who do not know them well, or seeing only a certain side of them, makes them appear more like the friends of the teens in your life.

My three children, for example, accept my friends. There have, however, been exceptions. One such exception is Ron. My children agree: Ron is the most obnoxious man they have ever met. They see him as negative, nagging, a whiner. When he and his family come to our home, he ignores my kids, treats his own kids with disrespect and treats his wife, who is a saint, like a stranger. He demands food and drink, eats a lot and leaves a mess everywhere. In spite of his wealth, he complains that he never has enough money. He clogs our toilet, expels gas and stinks up the house. Any wonder my kids cannot stand him? I try to explain to them that underneath all of that, I see good in Ron. They, in turn, think I need psychiatric treatment. But unlike my kids, I can see Ron struggling to be a better person. Ron is a gifted salesman, extremely bright in many areas, and generous to help a friend in need.

I similarly have had problems with some of my children's friends over the years. Ironically, they displayed many of the same characteristics as Ron! What were my kids seeing that I could not?

The point: be careful to criticize teenagers' good friends. It hurts them, just as it hurts you when they criticize your friends. You may be slamming the people who are their life line, their support. Their friends may not be model citizens, but our teens have seen their redeeming qualities—the beauty behind the ugliness, the beauty within. They recognize their friends' masks and can relate to the underlying pain. Our children understand what Jesus said: It will not be the righteous and the Pharisee who enter the kingdom of heaven, but the sinner and the tax collector.

We accept that our friends are alcoholic, abusive toward family members, ruthless in business, lazy, materialistic or wrapped up in secularism. We tolerate their eccentricities and make excuses for them. We convince ourselves that we will not be affected by their bad habits. So why do we not accept teens befriending people with similar problems? Perhaps our teens will be a good example for these kids and instrumental in changing their lives. The support, comfort, love and acceptance that teenage friendship provides pulls out the best in their friends ...and in the teens with whom we work and live.

Quick Tips

- Recognize how enriching teenagers' friendships are for them. Overlook the minor annoyances and appreciate the healing power of friends.
- Trust teenagers' choice of friends, especially when those choices are based on their intrinsic value, their inner beauty, loyalty and service. Expect that teens will see the greatness in their friends that we might miss.
- Focus on friendship's ability to reveal and nurture positive qualities among friends.
- Create situations in which teenagers can minister to each other. Empower them to help one another.

10: Who Created Their World?

Each generation of teens experiences their own joy and suffering, their unique good and bad times, their particular victories and failures. Looking back as adults, our experiences were neither harder nor easier, just different. We tend, however, to either glamorize our own "suffering youth," recalling long lists of chores and reminding our teens of how often we "went without," or to romanticize the "simpler times" when we played made-up games using household objects, sipped lemonade under the old oak tree and sat around the dinner table swapping the day's stories with our parents. All of us experienced some of both of these, but the bottom line is that the teenage years of any generation are full of difficult changes, insecurity and tough decisions. Some of the challenges we faced are still real for today's teens; others have been replaced with new challenges. The old pleasures, both forbidden and allowed, still exist—some as we knew them, some in different forms. A kid then is a kid now, but time clouds our memory of what that was really like. Be cautious in drawing comparisons or contrasts.

I often hear parents talk about how spoiled teens are today with their high standard of living and expensive cars, computers and video games. When I hear such criticism I feel sorry for the kids. These luxuries and comforts can, in fact, bring discomfort and suffering. Many kids feel tremendous pressure to obtain all the "things" that other kids have, mistakenly measuring their value by what they and their family do or do not own. And the kids who have a great many materials possessions begin seeing their world through what they own, alienating themselves from their peers because they perceive that their peers do not "measure up." These kids, the ones who own so much, can feel the loneliest and least secure.

Quick Tips

- Before criticizing a teen's lifestyle, consider the role the adults in his or her life have played in fostering that lifestyle. Consider the ongoing role you play in fostering that lifestyle.
- Dealing with a negative behavior? Start by asking, "Where did this behavior come from? Where was it learned?"

Sadly, teens have rarely *chosen* these luxuries: well-intentioned parents provide them, filling their homes with material goods and creating the expectation of instant gratification and ever-increasing wealth. On top of that, adults pressure today's teens with high-powered marketing, viewing them as a single, vast, potential "market" ripe for exploitation; our consumerist world makes itself rich by feeding on its own children.

It makes no sense to blame the kids for the world in which they live; they have neither the power nor the autonomy to create such a world. Adults create this world! Adults make the violent movies, invent the violent computer games and condone violent solutions to life's problems. Adults make weapons and wars, fighting over boundaries and hating people of different races and religions. Adults foster unhealthy competition, biases and intolerance. Adults make cars go faster, manufacture alcohol and drugs and produce pornography. Adults create the sophisticated technology that keeps kids inside, glued to televisions and computers. Adults model toxic materialism, secularism and consumerism. Adults create a political system filled with greedy, self-seeking bureaucrats and an economic environment corrupting enough to turn a saint into a swindler.

When you are about to criticize the teens in your church, classroom or home, stop and ask yourself about the behavior or attitude you dislike at the moment—where has it come from? Who has taught them this? No behavior, belief or attitude is created in a vacuum; what factors created what you see and struggle with now? We may wish to confront the attitude or behavior causing the problem, but it helps to realize that before we criticize *them*, we may first need to criticize *ourselves*. Teens learned these behaviors, attitudes and lifestyles from us and other family members. We shape and mold the children in our families, churches and schools. As adults we have to take a fair share of responsibility for what we see in them.

Much of it starts at home. I hear parents complain that today's teens are too materialistic; then I visit their homes and see furniture so elegant and expensive that I fear to sit on it. I know parents who have built walk-in closets to accommodate their extensive clothing and shoe collections, who then wonder aloud why their teens seem so focused on accumulating "stuff." I hear parents say their kids are addicted to drugs and alcohol, only to discover that these parents are addicted to gambling and work. I hear parents complain that their children are obsessed with videos and computers, only to discover that their parents are equally obsessed with fancy cars and making money. Parents complain when their children cheat or "fudge the truth"; their kids watch them manipulate facts and figures when it comes to their business or income taxes. Parents complain about their children's intolerance, while at the same time discouraging their children from dating someone of another race or religion.

I remember taking my oldest son, four years old at the time, to a park festival, a multicultural event with people from all races, religions and cultures. At his request, I took him first to the face painting booth. They painted his face an array of colors, and he was ecstatic. We continued our walk through this festival, visiting the various pavilions.

Suddenly, my son shouted out to me, "Look, Dad, that whole family has their faces painted." I looked in the direction he pointed and found myself staring at a family of African-Americans. I turned bright red, but was immediately grateful for their understanding laughter.

Why had my son thought this family painted their faces? He had frequently seen African-Americans, not only on television, but also in our community. I concluded it was the uniqueness of the day's situation: he had just had his face painted; his "color" had suddenly changed; his looked different to himself. The different look of his face had "tuned him in" to notice the difference in other's faces.

I then asked myself the question: How often are we unnecessarily "tuning in" our children to differences in race and religion? How often to we go beyond acknowledging differences to judging and evaluating the differences? How much aggression and violence result?

Behind every child behaving inappropriately lies a story—a story of pain, of fear, of abuse, of rejection, of simple poor modeling. These stories are *our* stories, stories for us to own, stories for us to confront and face. No escape for us adults: we must accept the responsibilities that come with raising and educating our children. The story of Roger, in the next chapter, illustrates how the world we create can impact our kids in destructive ways.

Quick Tips

- Keep digging deeper; the identified problem a teen experiences may really be a symptom of something deeper and more fundamental.
- Teenagers perceive the world as they have been taught to perceive it. It may take a while for a teen to re-imagine the world as a potentially safe place filled with opportunities for greatness.

11: Roger's Story

Roger missed school three days out of every five for six weeks. As per school policy, the school secretary phoned his home whenever Roger did not attend. Roger intercepted every call, impersonating his father and informing the secretary that Roger was ill.

After eighteen absences, the school sent a letter to Roger's parents, confirming the absences and warning that, if he missed another five, he would lose all his credits for the year. Roger's father received and read the letter on an afternoon when school was still in session; he immediately called the school, only to discover that Roger was absent again.

A few days later, at his request, Roger's father met with all of Roger's teachers. We sat around a large, rectangular table, waiting for him to arrive. As he walked in, all talking ceased —all eyes focused on this imposing 280-pound man, dressed in his work uniform. He took his place at the head of the table and started speaking, abruptly and to the point: "I want to hear what each of you have to say about my son. I want to hear about how he has been acting like an ass, but before you do I want you to know that I caught my son at the arcade playing video games when he was supposed to be in school. That explained to my wife and me where all the change has been going that was disappearing from her purse and where he has been when he is absent from school. When I found him at the arcade, I caught him off guard and gave him a good shot in the face. I broke his nose and his glasses.

This should put an end to any more problems you may have with him in the future."

The silence around the table was deafening, the tension choking. The wave of sympathy for Roger remained unspoken. The father had set the tone, and amazingly, in spite of their sympathy for Roger, not one teacher spoke in his defense. Instead, they quickly began criticizing him.

I, meanwhile, felt stunned. How could this large man hit his own son like that? Roger was a very frail, physically weak, 14-year-old boy, easily weighing less than 95 pounds.

When my turn to speak came, I said, "Roger is a very innocent and good kid. He has a lot of gifts, and his addiction to the arcade is not the problem, but a symptom of something else. He should be in counseling; that way we can discover why Roger is avoiding school and spending so much time at the arcade."

My suggestion fell on the father's deaf ears.

So, without the benefit of structured counseling, I made it a point to get to know Roger better through informal contacts at school. He shared with me how out of place he felt, both at home and in school. At home, Roger's bedroom held a TV, a computer and video games—here he found refuge. In these games he felt a sense of belonging. Through video games, he escaped to a world where he had some autonomy and power over others, playing the tough guy and enjoying some control over his own destiny.

The world Roger lived in was not created by him—not the fear, nor the loneliness, nor the technology. Roger's parents created this world for him. Roger's parents, instead of spending time with him, found it easier to get rid of him in a world of technological anesthesia. They created this world for Roger, a world which Roger then used to escape from them.

Roger was one of those kids easily lost in the background— one who would not return for counseling and would not ask for outside help. His parents' inability to admit that their son might have a problem compounded the likelihood that he would never get the help he needed. This is not uncommon; a proud parent, especially one who at some deeper level probably recognizes that he or she is part of the problem, has a tough time admitting that their child may need help. So kids like Roger continue to "go with the flow" of life, no matter how unpleasant, to avoid even less pleasant consequences.

How to help life's "Rogers"? As educators, approach parents with sensitivity. Do not immediately suggest that they are part of the problem; instead, encourage them, perhaps for the first time, to see life through their teenager's eyes. Can they listen more gently, more openly, more attentively to what their teen is doing and saying? Help them to see their role as observer and co-counselor. Then, as their understanding grows, it may be possible to suggest possible changes in home life, perhaps even family counseling.

From the point of view of the "Rogers" themselves, you may be surprised to know that they *do* understand how difficult life is for their parents, and how much effort it takes for parents to change. Kids may be more forgiving of their parents than their parents are of them. Helping teens understand and articulate this can help them handle difficult home situations, even if change never comes. Generally, if parents are willing to admit their frailty and make honest efforts to change, their kids feel satisfied and grateful.

Lord, teach us to offer a hand of love to a straying child crying for help. Give us the courage to acknowledge our responsibility in the face of problems we see in our teens. Amen.

Quick Tips

- If for some reason parents are unavailable (or unwilling) to help the healing process, involve peers to help teens face and overcome problems.
- If dealing with addictions, educate yourself through printed or on-line resources and support groups. Problem behaviors may indicate addiction; address the addiction.

On Hobbies and Interests

When working both with teens and their parents, I stress the importance of hobbies and other special interests. Over and beyond school homework and household chores, hobbies offer a host of benefits:

- They help develop healthy minds and spirits.
- They keep teens interested in life.
- They stimulate creative thinking.
- They open teens to new possibilities.
- They uncover life passions.

Think of the activities that you enjoy most, the ones that seem to flow, taking you, for a time, outside of yourself and your daily worries into a place of joy, peace and meaning. Teens need this experience too.

Sometimes we who live or work with teens focus only on the future value of their free-time activities: Is there a financial advantage? Is this giving them an edge academically or socially? Let go of these practical concerns and let kids follow their hearts. Encourage them to immerse themselves in projects they love—computing, baseball, soccer, ballet, musical performance, collecting music, gardening, cooking, wood-working, bicycling, roller-blading, stamp collecting, assembling jigsaw puzzles, solving wordsearches, making models, painting, whatever. They are building skills and self-esteem, discovering who they are, testing their limits and exploring future possibilities.

Quick Tips

- Recognize the value of hobbies: developing the mind, building confidence, discovering new interests, advancing skills, etc.
- Encourage teens to explore a variety of possible hobbies and interests.
- As a class, a group or a family, plan outings that introduce teens to new experiences and ideas, for example, camps, museums, plays, concerts, athletic events, etc. Any given activity may spark a lifetime passion in a teen.

12: Understanding—Key to Helping

As I write these words, I type them on a computer keyboard. Do I understand how computers work, how what I type somehow ends up in printed form? Not really. I know just enough to get words on paper...and that little sometimes makes me dangerous around this sophisticated technology. Just ask my kids.

Those same kids know enough about this computer to maintain it, not only keeping it running, but even fixing it if something breaks down and becomes jumbled.

The less I understand about the inner workings of my computer, the less able I am to keep it in healthy working order, and the greater the likelihood that I will be unable to fix it if it suddenly stops functioning.

For me, my relationship to the family computer is an apt metaphor for life—and in particular for my relationship to the teens in my life: The less I understand them, the more difficult I find it to work with them, and the less likely it is that I can help them when something in their lives goes wrong.

Whether teaching, parenting or leading teens, we must understand where they are in life, what they feel and think, what they believe and dream, what frustrates them, frightens them, delights them. Without such understanding, we relate to their lives with the same clumsiness with which the computer-impaired among us stare at the bewildering electronic world that exists inside our computer cases. Our teens *need* us to understand them; without our understanding, they experience the world as hopeless and threatening. If they perceive us as understanding and caring, they turn to us for help when they feel uncertain or make mistakes. If they perceive us as out of touch and uncaring, they turn instead to others, especially those who have life skills no greater than their own, people who *do* understand them because they are like them— other teens, many who are themselves desperate, lonely and broken.

The first step, then, is opening our hearts and minds to understand teenagers. Talk with them. Listen to them. Connect with them when and where they are most alive: watch one of their favorite TV shows with them; learn to play one of their video games; let them pick a video and watch it together; go out for pizza and talk about school, friendship, faith, life. And all the time listen, without judgment. Just listen to learn.

Buy a magazine aimed at teens and read it through. What does it tell you about teen interests? dress? pasttimes? social life? Drop by your local bookstore or library and ask about recent books on teens. Get together with other parents or leaders of teens, swapping stories and insights. Perhaps consider reading and discussing a book together—maybe even this one!

The second step, as you continue to grow in your understanding of teens in general and those with whom you live and work in particular, is to find ways to communicate to them how much you appreciate them, respect their insights and value their company. Learn to say it, simply and directly:

- "I appreciate you."
- "I enjoy being with you."
- "I learn from you."
- "Thanks for your perspective...your help...your humor...your ideas..."

A thank-you card mailed to home, a note tucked into a schoolbook, a card left on a dresser, a phone message to be retrieved after school, an e-mail, a hug, a quick fast-food lunch together—think creatively and you discover limitless ways to honestly, consistently communicate to teens how much you care about and appreciate them. Simply ask yourself: "What helps *me* to feel appreciated? understood? respected? valued?"

Parents, at home your teen needs stability. Stability comes, not with wealth, but through continuous love, affection and availability. When parents fail to understand and love them, the world, in the perception of the teen, abandons them. Home is critical—every child's haven from the suffering, set backs and traumas of life.

One evening at about midnight I received a call from a young boy named David. He had just fought with his mother's new boyfriend. David and the boyfriend had never gotten along, so David lived with his father and stepmother—a stable arrangement, though with its own share of problems. David asked if he could come to my house for the evening. I suggested he get permission first from his mother. He ignored my advice and took a cab to my home. We sat in front of the house under my large oak tree, talking in the darkness. In those few hours, in the quiet of the evening, David opened my eyes to so much. At one point I asked him, "David, if you had three wishes, what would they be?"

He thought for a moment and then responded, "My first wish would be that my grandfather was still alive."

I considered that for a moment before asking, "Why?"

"Because he knew how to love," he responded.

"And your second wish?" I asked.

Quickly he answered, "That my grandmother was still alive."

"For the same reason?" I asked.

"Yes," he answered.

"And your third wish?"

He leaned forward for a moment, looking at the ground. After a short pause he answered, softly and sadly, "I wish I could turn back time with what I know now."

"To when and why?"

"Back to before my parents divorced, so I could tell them what they are

doing wrong with each other. If I could do that, then they would still be married today."

"So that is your third wish, really, to have your mother and father still married?"

"Yes. To be a family again."

"But you have a good family today with your father and step-mother," I suggested. "They treat you well and love you."

"Yes," he admitted. "But it's not the same...and it's not what I want."

Do we listen to the voice of our teenagers? Do we hear what is in their hearts? Are we willing to make the sacrifices necessary to continue the flow of affirmation and love? If not, we end up with a lost generation of teens turned adult whose worlds have been broken and whose beauty and greatness have been lost. We all lose: they lose as they turn to the streets to heal their brokenness; we lose because we are deprived of their inspiration, wisdom and joy. When we fail to listen, when we wrap ourselves in self-gratification, our churches, homes and schools become places of antagonism and confrontation. Our teens then turn to friends and the streets, to media and technology, to drugs and alcohol for comfort.

In the following chapter I share with you the story of Maria, a beautiful young girl abused by a father who had neither inkling of nor interest in his daughter's life, heart or spirit. Misunderstood to the extreme, Maria embarked on a near-fatal course of self-destruction.

Quick Tips

- Want to understand teens?
  - Open your heart completely.
  - Listen without judgment, with the desire to understand, not to advise or change.
  - Explore their interests: book, magazines, movies, videos, games, websites, etc.
- Enter into and share a teen's pain, and you will better hear and understand their lives.

13: Maria's Story

Maria's mother abandoned her when Maria was a child, leaving her to be raised by her abusive father, a drug addict and active alcoholic. Maria wanted to escape from home and find a new life. What would this "new life" be like? She had no idea, but she believed it existed and wanted to experience it. It had to be better than what she knew.

At the age of 16, Maria moved out, continuing in school and collecting welfare to pay her expenses. During this time, her father sobered up and quit using drugs. When welfare discovered that Maria's father had improved and could take her back, they ended her assistance.

Maria refused to go home. Too much damage had been done at the hands of her father, and, despite his recovery from drugs and alcohol, he remained abusive. A friend invited Maria to share her apartment, then introduced her to an easy way of making money—the "escort" business. Maria was told that she could make a lot of money by simply escorting lonely men to parties or having dinner with them. She soon discovered that considerably more was expected: Maria began her brief career as a "call girl." Six months later, she became pregnant and had an abortion.

At this point, Maria reached out for help. She contacted a women's shelter, and they took her in off the streets. Maria, her spirit broken, emotionally exhausted, filled with guilt and shame, found refuge and hope at the shelter. They helped her begin to put her life back together. In Maria's words, "They saved me."

I will never forget one of my conversations with Maria. She sobbed as she told me how dirty she felt because of her work as a prostitute, how guilty, ashamed and worthless.

"Maria," I said, "I am proud of you. I am proud that you wanted to make it on your own. What you did, you did to survive. It was not a reflection of the beauty that is within you. Who you are—the real Maria—is pure. You are pure because your heart is pure."

A month passed before I saw Maria again. In that brief time she progressed remarkably, improving academically and forming healthy, new friendships with other girls in the shelter. Her smile reflected growing inner innocence and peace; she had never smiled like this before! She began to forgive her father, and to see and acknowledge the beauty within herself. Maria's forgiving heart, so common even among teens with a lot to forgive, led her to a place of greater wholeness and peace.

I sometimes wonder what obstacles Maria and other kids like her will face as adults because of these cruel life experiences. Surely the abuse they suffer comes back to haunt them in one way or another. If they grew up believing they were unlovable, they push away those who love them. If they believe they are failures, worth nothing, they will sabotage potential successes in life. If they believe they are ugly or "dirty," they will avoid intimacy.

Pray with me that these experiences of pain will forge out of them greatness. Pray that the beauty in these kids will be revealed...to us, to their families, teachers and friends, and, above all, to themselves.

Lord, may the years to come be kinder to Maria, and may the scars of her past increase her greatness. Lift all your children when they fall; strengthen them when they feel weak; open their eyes to beauty when all they see around them is ugliness. Heal their shattered lives. Amen.

Quick Tips

- Help teens forgive themselves by helping them understand that:
  - God forgives and accepts them, unconditionally;
  - you forgive and accept them, unconditionally.
- Focus on the inner spirit, faith and beauty of teens, not on external actions that may not reflect their rich inner life.

On Trusting Teens

Do you trust the teens with whom you work or live? Not if you view them as immature, unaware and ignorant. But are they?

I have dealt with many teenagers, who, in their short lives, have experienced more than many adults over the course of entire lifetimes. I find, in fact, a certain maturity among teens that comes from their freedom from the materialism that traps many in the adult world. But we tend to treat them (and others in life, by the way) the way we view them.

Imagine your boss calling you "stupid" or "a klutz" when you make a mistake. Imagine an older co-worker labeling you immature or childish. Imagine your office manager disciplining you by grounding you for a week. None of these approaches work when we deal with adults. They are not much more effective with teens. Kids, like adults, experience honest, everyday problems and make legitimate mistakes. They respond to criticism and discipline as sensitively as adults. Every time we approach teenagers to correct a mistake we can ask ourselves, "Is this how we would speak to a fellow adult? Is this the way we would like to be spoken to?"

We often base our approach to people on their status, position and power. Consequently, we tolerate much more from people who have power over us. We have power over teenagers; do we therefore sometimes treat them as "less than"? Although we are their leaders and teachers, parents and guardians, they deserve no less respect than our spouse at home, peer at work or associate in the community.

Teenagers commonly complain to me about this. They get along with their parents or teachers, but generally believe that these same people look down on them. They hear it in the tone of voice, choice of words and in the nature of discussion. This cultivates insecurity and undermines their self-confidence.

How can we demonstrate our trust in teens? Risk giving them the autonomy, authority and freedom they need to develop a stronger sense of them-selves. Express your faith in them and find oppor-tunities for them to live out their gifts and talents.

Quick Tips

- As parents, teachers, advisors and leaders, we offer direction to teens. Even as we do so, however, we are their equals, not their betters. Treat teenagers with the full respect and digni-ty with which you would like to be treated.
- Listen to teenagers' ideas and suggestions with an open mind; expect them to make great contributions.
- Remember: in their short lives, many teens have experienced more pain and heartache—more life—than many adults.

14: Patience

We all go through difficult times in our lives. In spite of the pain, hard times sometimes can be a gift and a blessing. Like the blacksmith who forges steel in the fire to create a wonderful tool, so the fires of life forge out of us great character. Pain humbles us, and with humility come wisdom and depth. Suffering invariably makes us more empathetic, compassionate, wise and prudent. Think about challenging times in your own past; can you see now how, through these painful experiences, God helped you to become more selfless and loving? The trauma or tragedy in itself is not the gift, but teenagers can understand that it is what they take, make, discover and create from the pain that makes the pain a gift. Life neither works out the way it should nor the way we want to. But as I explain to these teenagers, life works out best for those that make the best of the way things work out.

I encourage kids who are going through difficult times to embrace their pain, finding in their suffering whatever lesson may be there for them. All of us, adult and teen alike, have a choice: run from pain or embrace it. Many run by turning to drugs, alcohol or promiscuity. We can also escape in our work or hobbies, constantly keeping busy. Eventually, if we survive the flight (and some do not), we realize: there is no escape! We can bury the pain temporarily, but it always works its way out.

How do you embrace the pain? I tell teens to take the pain in their arms and hold it like someone they love. Take it on as Jesus did in the garden. Hold it close, feel it, breathe it, live it. Let it become, fully, a part of you. Then, with time and prayer, love and support, the pain diminishes, dwindling from a raging fire to the flicker of a candle, a candle that no longer threatens, but offers light and understanding. This is what it means to embrace pain and learn from it. This is how pain transforms us and enriches us, keeping us from hurting others and ourselves.

I also tell teens that one key to survival is *patience*. Once they acknowledge the need to reconnect with themselves, with others, with God and with family in healthy ways, I know that they will find the strength for the long journey to wholeness. Healing takes time, but it will come. It rarely comes quickly; step by step, insight by insight, they slowly discover their own inner beauty and the miraculousness of life. They begin to realize how much they offer to the world.

Quick Tips

- Be patient with teens.
- Teach teenagers to be patient with others, with the world, with life circumstances and with themselves.

Just recently I saw Lydia, a beautiful girl I counseled several years earlier, helping her through tremendous difficulty in her life. Lydia's mother had a "secret" lover, although Lydia was fully aware of the situation. She believed her father also knew, but that he chose to remain in denial and allow this continued affair. Clandestine phone calls, late-night rendezvous, erratic behavior—these drove Lydia crazy as her mother dehumanized her father and destroyed the family life Lydia once knew. Lydia turned her hatred of her mother inward, and it resulted in depression and thoughts of suicide.

In the face of such pain, how can a teen like Lydia believe that things will improve, that she will one day find peace? I tell kids repeatedly who suffer depression, "You have to believe this will end. Be patient. Just get through each day as it comes." Yes, the depression is deep and life dark and painful. Yes, it feels like it will never end. But it does end. "At the end of this dark tunnel is a light. When you arrive there, this light shines like you never imagined. This rain in your life makes you able to appreciate the sun when it shines again." Share this message of hope with depressed teens. Encourage them to be gentle and patient with life, no matter how badly it treats them. Eventually, life will be gentle and patient with them.

When Lydia and I met again, she embraced me and said, "You were right about patience." As we talked, I realized that her smile told it all—Lydia had endured and not given up. She had become a woman filled with happiness, enthusiasm and ambition.

I saw this with another wonderful kid named Jack, a major behavioral problem, a poor student and, according to every one of his teachers, headed for a life of failure and disaster. Throughout our years of counseling, I repeatedly told Jack that his life would change for the better if he believed in himself and was patient: "You are going to be a great success in life! Just wait; you *will* get through this, and it will be good." I believed it absolutely; I could see it in him. Ten years have passed, and Jack is now a regional manager for a major international company.

If our teens can just hang on through the difficult times, they will share their gifts with the world. We increase their chances when we too are patient with them, expressing our undying belief in them, empowering them, opening opportunities to them, and, above all, loving them. They will make it. They will give back to the world the wonderful talents and gifts that God gave to them.

Our teenagers really do not ask for much out of life—just some love, respect and autonomy. When we do not provide these, teens look elsewhere, often in places that potentially could destroy them. Meet these simple needs, and we will see a generation of children grow up to make their dreams come true and create a better world.

I have seen the light shine in our teens, even in their darkest moments. I end this book with a story of a girl who, even in her darkest times, could see the love of her Father in heaven. Her deep spirituality, buried under a sea of pain, abuse and darkness, is an example of what has inspired me in working with teenagers. I give thanks to God for bringing me to this place in my life.

Quick Tips

● Help teens see the ways that pain and suffering may serve a greater purpose. As you do so, never minimize or discount their pain.
● Encourage teens to consider that what they learn from difficult times will equip them to help others later in life.
● When helping victims of abuse, continually remind them that it is not their fault.

15: Samantha's Story

Like flowers awaiting spring rain, teens' greatness blossoms when showered with genuine concern and compassion. Samantha desired to be loved, yearned to believe she was lovable. Not much to expect from life? For girls like Samantha, love is hard to find. Those spring rains may never come. When raised to believe they are unlovable, our kids live in darkness and despair; nothing in life carries the promise of new life. They bury the pain and brokenness in drugs, crime, promiscuity and suicide. Samantha, like many teenagers, resorted to anything to get the love she needed. Yet even in the winter of her life, waiting for some promise of spring and the possibility of healing, nurturing rain, she still caught glimpses of God's love.

A guidance councilor approached me about Samantha, wanting me to see her because she had attempted suicide. It was not her first attempt. I immediately found her in class and escorted her to my office.

The kids know that when I come to get them it is because I want to talk to them about some problem they are having. They are cooperative and usually feel happy that I have come for them. In fact, with the hundreds of kids that I have retrieved over the years, not one has resisted the invitation to speak to me. Kids trust. They are willing to give each new "messiah" a chance at helping solve their problems.

I began my session with Samantha like I do with most of the teens, starting with comfortable, easy-to-answer questions. I ask questions that help them feel good about themselves and, hopefully, at ease with me. From there I move to questions dealing with ethnic background, family background, school history, places they have been, and hobbies and activities they enjoy. These questions build our initial relationship, and provide a window into the hearts and minds of the kids. Through it all, I hope that each teen will provide the opening needed to enter into the more critical issues. Such is what I did with Samantha.

I found Samantha to be lethargic about life. She had lost the typical teenage zest and enthusiasm. She found nothing in life worth loving, least of all herself. This led me to get directly to the reason I called her down to my office; I told her that guidance had informed me of her suicide attempts. I asked, "Why do you want to destroy such a beautiful person as yourself?"

"I find it difficult to believe I am beautiful."

There are many kids like Samantha. They believe they are not *worth* loving. A lot of damage has been done to them. Abandoned or abused by parents—whom these teens believe are the only true yardstick of their worth—they develop an insecurity so powerful it leads to a life of pain, chaos and self-destruction. I can only remind them, repeatedly, "You *are* beautiful. You *are* valuable. You *are* lovable." They know that I am sincere; they hear it in my voice and see it in my eyes. *Although they do not believe it about themselves, they believe that I believe it.*

I can't really explain why, but no matter how severe the damage, no matter what they have done, I see such great beauty in these kids. I see their endless reservoir of potential. All I have to do is read between the lines, look into their eyes and listen to their broken voices. Do the same, and you too will see their beauty—the beauty of their innocence, their infinite potential and their deep spirituality.

Samantha showed me the marks on her wrist, grim testimony of her repeated suicide attempts. Like many kids who try it, she intended to be unsuccessful at suicide and planned such attempts so that she would be discovered, listened to and helped. I took her hand and spent a few moments silently staring at the marks. I then rubbed my fingers gently over the scars. I said how disturbed I was to see and feel them. We talked, softly, about her attempts to end her life.

After an hour of sharing these experiences with a stranger, showing him the marks of hatred towards herself, Samantha felt worn out. Deciding whether or not to end the session at this point was difficult, because we were just about to explore the most critical issues. At times like these, I need to trust my instincts: What feels right? Stopping now, will the moment be lost? Is the teen, though tired, at the verge of a major, powerful breakthrough? Or could I continue later, trusting that groundwork has been laid for a future meeting?

Though she was tired, I believed that now was Samantha's time. She did not really want to kill herself. She was crying out to the world and had something important to say. She had not yet said it, but she was ready. This was the critical moment; I could feel it; I decided to continue.

A few moments later, Samantha told me about her incestuous relationship with her father. The relationship had come to light in part due to Samantha's revealing it, and Samantha had been placed in foster care while her father was placed under a restraining order. Samantha, however, still saw her father. They met after school. He would bring her to a remote place where she would satisfy him sexually. He would then leave her at a bus stop to return home to her foster parents.

I asked Samantha, "Why do you continue to do this?"

"Because I need his love. I have nobody else."

I hesitated, shaken. I stared at the top of her head, now hung low, out of guilt? shame? "Samantha, you don't have to do that for love. You have a Father in heaven who loves you infinitely just for who you are."

At that, she lifted her head, looked into my eyes and began crying uncontrollably. I took her into my arms and held her as she sobbed.

I counseled Samantha regularly after that initial visit. And I am certain there will be a special pace for Samantha in God's kingdom, both here on earth and in heaven.

Samantha has lived with Christ the crucifixion.

And the time will come when she will experience the resurrection.

Lord, let the light of your love shine bright on these your children. Only through your love will their cold world once again be warm, and they will return to you and blossom with all the gifts you so generously gave to them. Amen.

Quick Tips

- Remind the teens in your life that they are beautiful and of infinite worth.
- Emphasize for teenagers the great love God has for them.
- When talking with teens, always be sincere. Empathize—feel with them the things they feel.
- Freely share your love and concern for teens. Let them know you enjoy their company, value their input and respect their thoughts and feelings.

Conclusion

Dear Reader,

Thank you for walking this journey with me. I hope the stories of these teens help you, as they do me, see their remarkable beauty. They are the source of my greatest joy in life, because in *their* faces, I see the face of God.

Sincerely,

Peter Tassi